And Now My Wrist Hurts - A Collection of Poems

Aria Oakbelle

Presentation by *BookLeaf Publishing*

Web: www.bookleafpub.com

E-mail: info@bookleafpub.com

ISBN: 9789357614917

First edition 2022

*To my fiancé Adam, my best friend and
sister Astra, and my role model and big
brother Jonny: the three people who always
believed in me and got me here.*

ACKNOWLEDGEMENT

I'm bad at these things, but firstly I have to thank my amazing other half Adam. In our world he's known as Leo, and he has been my rock for so many years now. Without him I couldn't have started down this path, let alone got this far, so thank you, from the bottom of the ice queen's heart haha.

Friends are the family we choose for ourselves, and I have such an amazing family and community I've built along with Astra the past few years. To her, to Waffles, to all those friends that are family out there who have supported me, thank you. Your love and support has kept me going through dark times, and without you guys there is no House Oakbelle.

Then there's Jonny, who I have to single out for the reason that he is the guy who initially pushed me to go for my degree, as well as teaching me so many things (including a few things he probably didn't intend to). I couldn't have wished for a better role model to look up to, and I just hope to do you proud.

I also have to thank BookLeaf Publishing for giving me this opportunity and letting someone as mad as me jump on board. They are amazing and this couldn't have been put together without them. Also thank you to my tutors from the Open University that guided me through my degree and dealt with all my madness.

PREFACE

So... my first published work. Madness really. I'm not really sure what I should put here, it's not like there is a theme here or any sort of process other than trying to go for it and going for it. Poetry was the first thing I started writing as a kid, and although I've dipped in and out over the years I've always felt a strong pull to the rhythmic nature of verse, so here we are!

I will admit, that throughout my life I've endured some hardships and struggled a lot with mental health issues, and some of the poems in this collection will reflect that, but I also hope to sprinkle in some joy and a little nonsense now and then as well. Some of the entries are sad and depressing, but that's okay, because that's life. Take the bad with the good, the despair with the hope, everything in balance.

This collection is a little of everything, and the forms and the writing may not be perfect, but the beauty of poetry is that it doesn't have to be. I hope you enjoy at least some of the poems in here, and remember one and all to believe in yourself. As my mum always used to say when we were kids: 'Do as I say, not as I do!'

Welcome

Twenty-one poems:
Tasked with writing one a day.
Well, here's my effort!

My Dream

When I was young, I loved to read
Winnie-the-Pooh, Alice, my best friends indeed.
I loved the fantasy, the magic, the lore,
all I could read and yet always wanting more.
Blyton and Pratchett, even Rowling,
each entry released would make my heart sing
but no matter how many pages I turned,
no matter how much I read, I never could learn
why no one I saw was ever like me,
why those with troubles could never be free.
I saw vampires and witches, the good and the
bad,
how evil is made, not born, and the reasons
always sad.
Betrayal and loss, never-ending sorrow,
yet only the perfect getting the better tomorrow.
So I made a promise, a solemn vow,
that I'd introduce us to the world somehow:
the loners and misfits, the ones who are lost,
the ones whose happiness shouldn't be the cost
to give the "good" and the "heroes" their happy
end,
that we're capable of love and being a friend.
Now here I am, making my first attempt
to write professionally, even though I feel inept.

To showcase the odd, the sad, and the weird
so others can know that we're not to be feared;
that just because someone has struggles or pain
doesn't mean you should leave them out in the
rain.
Please, take the bad with the good, the strong
with the weak,
then maybe there'll be some of the balance we
seek
where we are judged by our actions and words
but WITHIN the context of how we all were
hurt.
Now that I'm older, I still love to read,
but Eeyore and Caterpillar make more sense to
me.
Some villains have their reasons, not all heroes
are good
and all each want, all everyone wants, is to be
understood.

#ENVTubers

Set up OBS
Tech is working, okay…
Remember to load the game dummy!
Easy listening music ready for starting soon
Activating stream mode:
Model loaded and moving?
I think I'm ready?
Now or never
Go go go!

Very nice physics you have
Take your eyes off the jiggle!
Under no circumstances do you lewd!
Beware the witch's fire
Everyone else, welcome ^^
REEE! I'm not cute, you are!

Random Thought

5

Sometimes I find my brain shall say,
on any random or given day,
that it has simply gone away.
And I try to go about my day
hoping my brain won't stay away,
but when a friend around will say
'I just need a random word, okay?'
I am, without a doubt, in a way,
about to say:
Yoghurt.

Bullies

You call me weird like it's an insult.
Geek and dork, strange and odd,
like these are bad traits to be forgotten.
Just because I have interests and loves
you'd laugh, cast me out, look down from
above.
But who wants to be "normal", really?
Dull and boring, desperately needy.
You require approval, respect from others,
I found my people, they're other fandom lovers.
So call me teacher's pet, call me gay,
call me every name in your limited vocabulary,
because it's not an insult.
And at the end of a long day,
you'll be turning to me to say:
'Do you want fries with that?'

For Adam

There is one who happens to be
all the parts that are missing from me.
He wrote one first,
so I copied his verse
to see him smile when he reads.

A Note Left On A Clifftop

As I sit here in the rain,
pain, plain on my face, feel my heart race
as drops fall in place
of the tears I should be crying if I wasn't already
dying
on the inside.

Bound behind a broken mask,
hard task, I ask should I be this way yet another
day
or just fade away
from this life where I'm lying and constantly
dying
on the inside.

When all I want is to hurt,
subvert, convert pain to blood, a devastating
flood
of emotion shoved
deep down and I'm just trying to keep my dying
on the inside.

Surrounded by darkness of night,
no light, frighteningly similar to my soul, no
longer whole

as I paid the toll
for their crimes, confining me to dying
on the inside.

All I see in their eyes is hate,
can't wait, too late to change this path, as they
laugh
and I'm starved
of what could help me in denying that I'm dying
on the inside.

Now I stand here in the rain,
again, pain etched on my face, feel my pulse
race,
as I fall with grace
and land with a sigh, relying that I'm dying
on the outside.

My Star

My best friend is an amazing girl
with friends and knowledge from all over the
world,
but she thinks so little of herself
that I wanted to give her a bit of help.
Younger than me, yet I admire her so,
her passion, determination, ability to grow.
All she wants is to help one and all,
will take on anything, no matter how small.
Training to be a future M.D.,
she means everything to the community and me.
She doubts herself, but she should know,
her light makes everyone else glow.
I hope she sees how bright she can shine,
that talented, devoted, Star of mine.

Stolen Main

Overwatch, Apex, Mario Party,
Monster Prom, Mary-Kate and Ashley,
fighting over who is who
hoping the first one to pick is you.
Others taking the one you love
making you swear to heavens above:
'They better play as good as me!'
and having to pick option B or C.
The game starts, goes on, you have to play,
you want to blow the thief away,
you play your best, they do the same,
(even if you have to play someone you think is
lame)
then either way, it comes to an end,
win or lose, against foe or friend.
GG, tough loss, then we all move on,
but next time? They're mine! Disconnect and
we're gone.

Best Girls And Boys

12

What is a Waifu?
Your best and most favourite
of fictional girls.
So…
What's a husbando?
It's the same of course, silly,
this time it's the guys.
Characters that we adore
and will stan forever more.

Our Wolf Boi

Our stinky wolf boi hit 1 million
who would have seen it coming?
We, the community, of course!
To us it was always certain.
The way you work so very hard
to make us love and laugh
and all the effort you have made
to perfect your craft
meant we never had a single doubt,
we had belief, we knew,
that no matter how hard or dark the days
our wolf boi would see us through.
Father, brother, mentor, friend
you're something to us all,
holding us, supporting us,
until we all stand tall.
No one deserves this more than you,
of that we all are sure,
so here to you and those 1 million subs
and many millions more.

Thankful For Rain

There's a mask of smiles that hides their pain
as they gratefully stand in the misty air.
No one can see them crying in the rain.

Every day for them an emotional drain,
a never-ending internal nightmare
forcing the mask of smiles to hide their pain.

Thankfully the heavens open again,
cold droplets of water that conceal the despair.
'They can't see I'm crying in the rain.'

All they want is their brain to refrain
from causing more damage, and needing repair
to the mask of smiles that hides their pain.

There's never a way to show or explain
the why or the how. They can only declare
that they aren't crying, it's just the rain.

Outside in the downpour, they need no longer
restrain,
they don't have to care, be aware, or beware.
Through the mask of smiles that hides their pain,
no one can see you're crying in the rain.

Witching Hour

15

Upon a darkened night when skies are clear
of all but stars and the full moon up high,
magic, ghosts, and mysteries all are near
for the witching hour is coming by.
Power flowing, sizzling through the air
as the witches and familiars start
to prepare their spells and cast them with care
with an open mind and a loving heart.
Good luck and good wishes, all that we send,
those doing otherwise soon to regret
for all we put out comes back in the end
by the rule of three, what you give, you get.
So be nice, be good, whether witch or not:
Deeds done that hour will not be forgot.

Kitteh

Shake the rain from meow fur
euch, water is wet.
Backdoor is closed,
find the open window aaaaand…
POUNCE!
Hi humeown!
Headbutt
Feed meow!
Headbutt
Fluffy socks! Wind round legs
hisssssss mind meow tail!
Feed and love meooooooow!!
No, do both at once.
Nom nom nom.
Back out window
This is meow area!
Random kitteh?
Fight to protect humeown!
Strut home after win
'Have you been fighting again?'
Silly humeown,
only to protect yous!

Tombola

Deposit, then play.
Only staked what can afford
bingo or arcade.
It's fun to play, but really,
a win would be nice please Bob!

The Waffley-Man

There's a streamer who goes by
Waffles4Chumps
who never leaves anyone down in the dumps,
his face always smiling and calm on the cam
old friends and new, he don't give a damn.
Everyone gets a 'hello' and a smile,
even if he forgets about chat once in a while.
Gambling, horror, cults and space,
the madness we quote that comes out his face:
"Oh, he's down! Get his butt! Get his butt!"
"We gotta yaba daba do those drugs!"
"Where are the boobies? I must consult them."
"Oh that's the turn and run bitch button!"
"If only someone had licked me! That would've
solved our problems!"
"Just let me dropkick babies in peace! I don't
wanna know their names"
"Nothing weird here, taste the walls! Taste your
friends!"
"People come from miles to rub my head!"
"I really gotta think before I say stuff..."
"We're going to get to 500 quotes of
out-of-context terribleness!"
"I'm the smartest smartie smart that ever
smarted"

"Am I dumb chat? Wait... don't answer that..."
"I've never said anything stupid!"
"I'm a dumb American, we don't know Europe!"
"My sexiness will get me through this."
"Why does nothing die when I kill it?!"
"He was my friend and lover and I murdered him"
"Don't reward me for sucking!"
"Note to self - equip spacesuit before jettisoning yourself into space..."
And the one we hear most of all: "Waffles has made mistakes."

Gone

Left out in the cold,
alone, lost and forgotten
abandoned in the basement
of the house where
we used to live.
'Gone.' they said when I returned,
'Given to charity for some
poor soul to call their own.'
I weep for that long-lost toy
And my childhood that was lost with it.

Escape

I wasted so much
time on you I can't get back.
Glad I got away.

Magic Has A Price

There was a world of legends long ago
where Kings and Queens reigned from castles on
high,
all peoples were free to go to and fro, and
it seemed that their happiness would never run
dry.
But then Uther Pendragon started a war
just because he didn't want to pay the price
of magic he begged another to cast
even though she had warned him: a life costs a
life.
So witches and healers, all who did good
were forced into hiding, hoping not to be found,
he called them all evil, wicked and rotten,
and persuaded his people they belonged in the
ground.
Druids took to the forest, others tried to run
to kingdoms far away,
but Uther's hatred reached even there and
caused some who were good to sway
to the darker side of magical arts;
the ones that can cause pain and death,
and all because Uther was determined to hunt
them all, to their or his last breath.
What happened next… most stories differ

on whether Arthur took the side
of his father, and continued hunting
those who were forced to hide.
Or if he kept an open mind
and allowed himself to think
for himself for once in his life,
on whether the whole system was a weak link.
But no matter what the story,
In the end, Uther's hubris led to the fall
Of Camelot,
The greatest city of legends of them all.

Scuffstra and Friends

There's one who goes by Scuffstra online,
her streams entertaining every time.
She tries her best to include all of chat
whether talkers or lurkers, she don't care 'bout
that.
Now and then, then tech won't play ball
but fun times can still be had by all
and that's when the madness really can start
and we quote all that's said that isn't that smart:
"So just type enterme and that's all... just enter
me..."
Waffles said: "They kept spitting their white goo
at me!"
"Do your job and remind me that I gotta fix my
tits!!"
"I want a butt massage!" – Waffles. She said
"Pay for it!"
"Yes I am the poker, I scare Entertain with my
big dicks!"
"Can I loot the living person?"
"It's not going up!"
"She just kept poking my butt!"
'Waffles is the luckiest boi, he gets to sit on my
booba!!'
"Even if it's hard, you have to endure."

Then everything goes dark and it's usually sudden,
until we hear in the distance: "I pressed the wrong button!"
But soon she's back to yell, with everyone else in tow,
"I'm not cute, just fluffy! (but I am fucking precious tho)"

Goodbye

Twenty-one poems:
Tasked with writing one a day.
This was my effort.
Somehow, I got through it all
Thanks for reading my madness.

www.ingramcontent.com/pod-product-compliance
Lightning Source LLC
La Vergne TN
LVHW051245200726